INSTRUMENTAL Solotrax

VOLUME **7**

SACRED SOLOS FOR FLUTE OR VIOLIN

Arranged by Marty Parks

The flute/violin solo folio is only temporarily stapled to the center of the book.
It is easily removed by a slight outward pull.

Lillenas PUBLISHING COMPANY
Kansas City, MO 64141

CONTENTS

	Piano	Flute/Violin
BE EXALTED	5	4a
Be Exalted, O God		
The Heavens Declare		
Be Thou My Vision	51	18a
Do You Know My Jesus?	63	22a
GLORIOUS IS THY NAME	36	14a
Glorious Is Thy Name (Mozart)		
Glorious Is Thy Name (McKinney)		
GOODBY, WORLD, GOODBY	43	16a
Goodby, World, Goodby		
When the Roll Is Called Up Yonder		
In the Presence of Jehovah	25	10a
Just Over in the Gloryland	32	12a
Lord, I Lift Your Name on High	58	20a
My Wonderful Lord	13	6a
OUR GREAT SAVIOR MEDLEY	18	8a
Our Great Savior		
Lord, We Praise You		
Praise God, from Whom All Blessings Flow		
THE HONORS OF THY NAME	68	24a
O for a Thousand Tongues		
Blessed Be the Name		
TRAVELING ON	75	26a
I Feel like Traveling On		
We'll Work Till Jesus Comes		

Be Exalted

Be Exalted, O God
The Heavens Declare

Arranged by Marty Parks

With strength ♩ = ca. 96

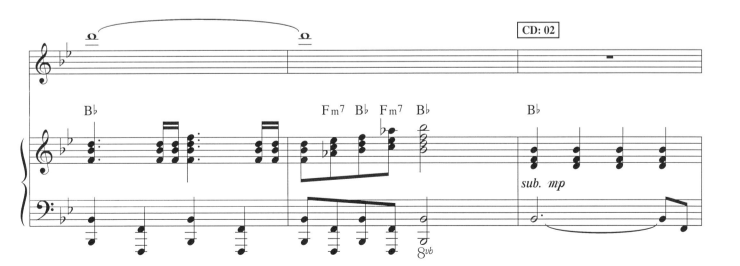

6

11 *"Be Exalted, O God"

*"The Heavens Declare"

My Wonderful Lord

HALDOR LILLENAS
Arranged by O.D. Hall, Jr.
Solo arrangement by Marty Parks

CD: 08

14

Our Great Savior Medley

Our Great Savior
Lord, We Praise You
Praise God, from Whom All Blessings Flow

CD: 14

Arranged by O.D. Hall, Jr.
Solo arrangement by Marty Parks

With strength ♩= ca. 104

CD: 15 1st time

CD: 17 2nd time

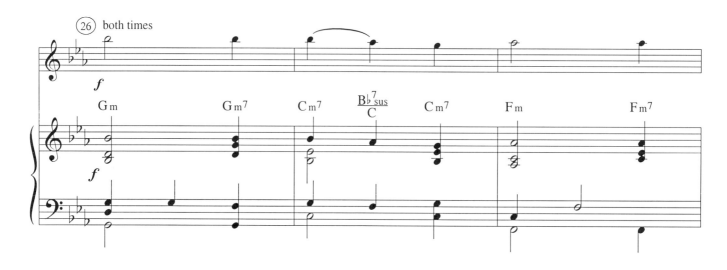

46 *"Lord, We Praise You"

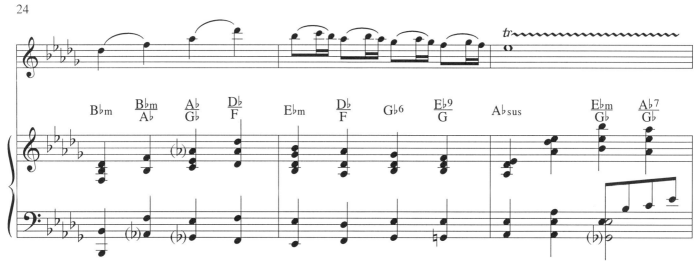

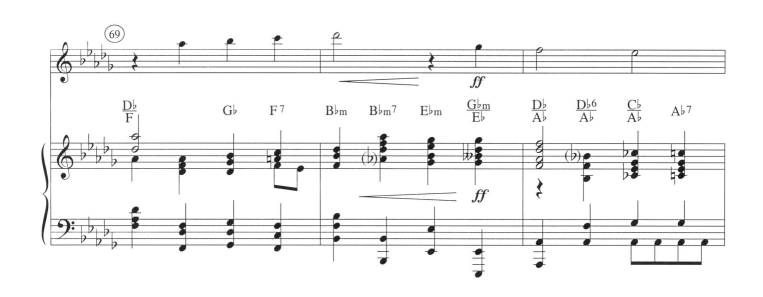

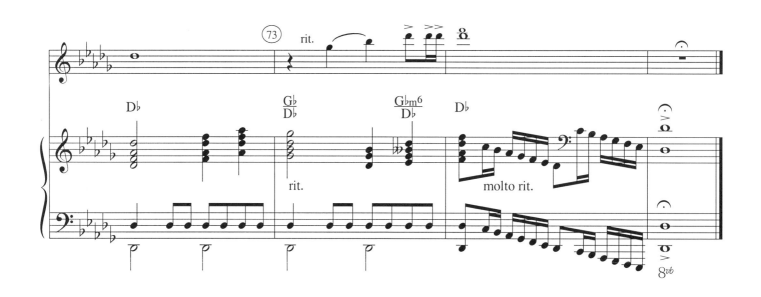

In the Presence of Jehovah

GERON DAVIS
Arranged by Marty Parks

Just Over in the Gloryland

EMMET S. DEAN
Arranged by O.D. Hall, Jr.
Solo arrangement by Marty Parks

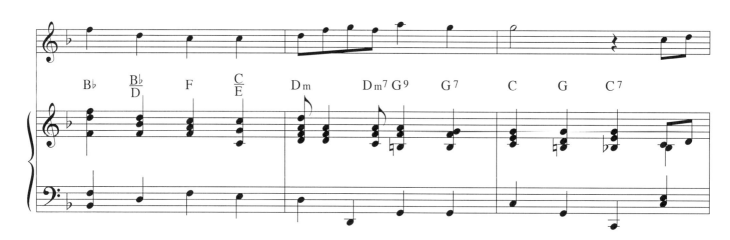

34

Glorious Is Thy Name

Glorious Is Thy Name (Mozart)
Glorious Is Thy Name (McKinney)

Arranged by Tom Fettke
Solo arrangement by Marty Parks

With majesty ♩ = ca. 122

CD: 31 *"Glorious Is Thy Name"

③

38

Goodby, World, Goodby

MOSIE LISTER
Arranged by Camp Kirkland
Solo arrangement by Marty Parks

With energy ♩ = ca. 126

CD: 35

46

48

*"When the Roll is Called Up Yonder"

Be Thou My Vision

Traditional Irish Melody
Arranged by Tom Fettke
Solo arrangement by Marty Parks

52

Lord, I Lift Your Name On High

RICK FOUNDS
Arranged by Marty Parks

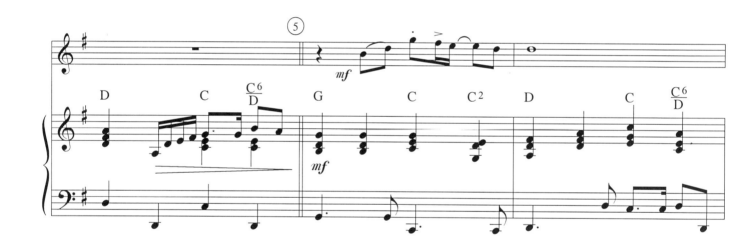

62

Do You Know My Jesus?

W.F. (Bill) LAKEY
and V.B. (Vep) ELLIS
Arranged by Mosie Lister
Solo arrangement by Marty Parks

66

The Honors of Thy Name

O For a Thousand Tongues
Blessed Be the Name

With great intensity ♩= ca.92

Arranged by Tom Fettke
Solo arrangement by Marty Parks

"O For a Thousand Tongues" (Carl Glazer)

Traveling On

I Feel Like Traveling On
We'll Work Till Jesus Comes

Arranged by Tom Fettke
and Randy Smith
Solo arrangement by Marty Parks

Joyous ♩ = ca. 72

CD: 60

"I Feel Like Traveling On" (Anonymous)

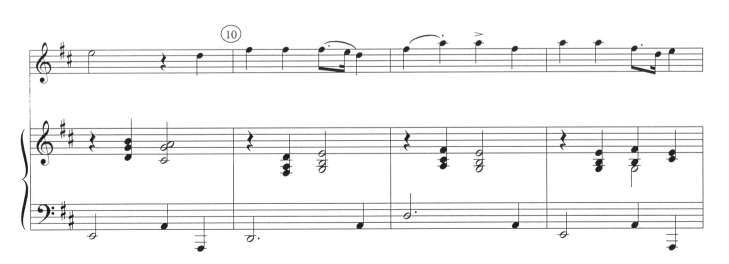

"We'll Work Till Jesus Comes" (William Miller)
play cued notes 2nd time

(to pg. 78, meas. 55)